THE

SPACE HERO

COOKBOOK

BARBARA BEERY

PHOTOGRAPHS BY
LISETTE DONADO

FAMILIUS

Published by Familius LLC, www.familius.com

Familius books are available at special discounts
for bulk purchases for sales promotions or for
family or corporate use. Special editions, including
personalized covers, excerpts of existing books, or
books with corporate logos, can be created in large
quantities for special needs. For more information,
contact Premium Sales at 559-876-2170
or email specialmarkets@familius.com.

Library of Congress Catalog-in-Publication Data
2015940074
ISBN 9781942934004

Edited by Lindsay Sandberg
Photography by Lisette Donado
Cover and book design by David Miles

10 9 8 7 6 5 4 3 2 1

First Edition
Printed in China

CONTENTS

CRAFTS

CHIPS, DIPS & SNACKS

GREEN GALAXY DIP

INGREDIENTS

1 avocado, peeled and pitted

1/4 cup whipped cream cheese

1 tablespoon lemon juice

1 tablespoon honey

MAKES 1 CUP

1 Place all of the ingredients in a bowl or zip-close plastic bag and mash together.

2 Serve with Star Dust Pita Chips (page 8), chopped veggies, fruits, crackers, or pretzels.

For extra fun, smash the ingredients together by hand in a plastic bag.

The Green Galaxy was mistakenly called the Red Galaxy for over 150 years, until, in fact, the astute Arcanian Observatory discovered the splotch of ketchup on its telescope lens.

Postal services in the region are still sorting out the mess.

PITA CHIPS

1 Preheat the oven to 400 degrees. Line a cookie sheet with foil and set aside until ready to use.

2 Cut bread into desired shapes using a pizza wheel, cookie cutters, or scissors.

3 Brush the pieces of bread with olive oil, and sprinkle on sea salt and pepper.

4 Bake on prepared sheet pan for 5–7 minutes. Remove from oven and dust with edible glitter.

INGREDIENTS

3 large whole wheat pitas or flat breads

1 tablespoon olive oil

Sea salt and pepper, to taste

Edible glitter

MAKES APPROXIMATELY 20-30 CHIPS

Consuming stardust has no known ill side effects, but ingesting large quantities in conjunction with happy thoughts can induce unintended levitation. Please consult your doctor if these symptomns persist.

HYPERSPACE HUMMUS
WITH VOYAGER VEGGIES

INGREDIENTS

cups canned chickpeas, drained
nd rinsed

–3 medium beets, cooked or
asted, coarsely chopped

garlic clove, peeled and smashed

tablespoons lemon juice

/4 cup water

/2 teaspoon ground cumin

/2 teaspoon sweet paprika

live oil and flat-leaf parsley, for
arnish

MAKES ABOUT 2
UPS

1 Place the chickpeas and chopped beets in a food processor along with the garlic, lemon juice, and water. Pulse the mixture for about one minute. Add more water if needed to form a smooth and creamy consistency.

2 Add cumin and paprika and blend another 30 seconds to combine all ingredients.

3 Garnish with olive oil and flat leaf parsley, and serve with fresh veggie dippers, pretzels, and pita or tortilla chips.

SPACE HERO HELPFUL HINT:
Hyperspace Hummus makes a great lunch on whole grain flatbread or pita. Garnish with shredded carrots and sliced cucumbers.

> A word to the wise: It's best not to eat anything before traveling through hyperspace. Even your veggies.

ORBITAL ORANGE CARROT DIP

1 Cook carrots in water for 7–10 minutes or until fork tender. Drain and transfer to food processor.

2 Add oil, cumin, honey, lemon, and optional harissa, and pulse until smooth.

3 Season with salt and pepper, adding more lemon or honey to taste.

4 Garnish with shredded carrots and cucumbers.

SPACE HERO HELPFUL HINT:
Harissa is an aromatic paste made with chilies, garlic, cumin, caraway, coriander, paprika, and olive oil. It is used as a condiment and flavoring in the North African and Middle Eastern regions of Earth.

INGREDIENTS

4 large carrots, cut into 1-inch chunks

3 tablespoons olive oil

1 teaspoon ground cumin

2 teaspoons honey

Juice of 1 lemon

1 teaspoon mild harissa, optional

Sea salt and pepper

1/4 cup cucumber and carrots, shredded and combined, for garnish

MAKES 2 CUPS

BREADSTICK BLASTERS

INGREDIENTS

1 (1/4 oz) package yeast

1 tablespoon honey or pure maple syrup

1 cup warm water

1 1/2 cup white flour

1 1/2 cup whole wheat flour

1/2 cup grated Mozzarella cheese

1 teaspoon olive oil

Sea salt and pepper

1 teaspoon poppy or sesame seeds (optional)

MAKES 8 BREADSTICKS

Luck may favor the prepared, but there's nothing like a good breadstick at your side.

1 Combine yeast, honey or maple syrup, and warm water, and let set for 5–10 minutes until bubbles form.

2 Mix the flours together in a small bowl. Add the flour mixture to the yeast mixture 1/2 cup at a time, mixing well between each addition. Knead the dough a few times, then place in a bowl. Cover with a towel and place in a draft-free place, such as inside an oven or microwave (turned off) and allow the dough to rise 30–45 minutes.

3 Preheat the oven to 350 degrees. Line a baking sheet with parchment paper and spray lightly with cooking spray. Set aside until ready to use.

4 Remove dough from bowl and place on a flour-covered work area. Sprinkle the cheese on top and knead it into the dough until incorporated. Continue kneading dough until smooth.

5 Divide the dough into 8 balls and form each into a breadstick shape. Brush with olive oil and sprinkle with salt and pepper and optional seeds. Place on prepared baking sheet and bake for 8–10 minutes or until light golden brown.

6 Remove from oven and serve with Mars Marinara Sauce (page 26).

STARFIGHTER FRUIT KABOBS

1 Using a sharp knife, cut 12 watermelon cubes and 12 pineapple cubes into triangles.

2 To make a kabob, insert 1 pineapple triangle, followed by half of a kiwi, 1 watermelon cube, 1 cantaloupe cube, and finally 1 watermelon triangle. Repeat for other skewers until all fruit has been used.

INGREDIENTS

1 fresh pineapple, cubed

6 kiwis, halved and peeled

1 personal or small watermelon, cubed

1 cantaloupe, cubed with slightly tapered edges

12 8-inch wooden skewers

MAKES 12 FRUIT KABOBS

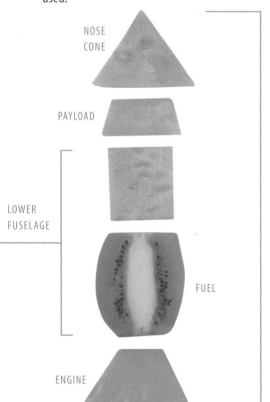

NOSE CONE

PAYLOAD

LOWER FUSELAGE

FUEL

ENGINE

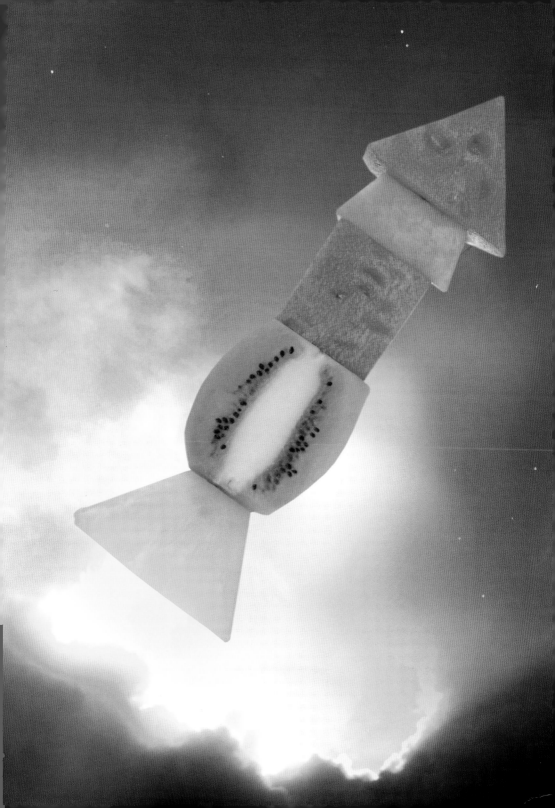

SECTOR 2

SAVORY

TURBO TOT ASTEROIDS

INGREDIENTS

2 cupcake liners

tablespoons extra virgin olive oil

/2 teaspoon salt

/2 teaspoon freshly ground black epper

/2 teaspoon sweet paprika

/2 teaspoon garlic powder

/2 teaspoon minced rosemary

2 baby potatoes, pricked with a ork

rated cheddar cheese, Greek ogurt, chopped green onions, and acon bits (optional)

MAKES 24 "TOTS"

1 Preheat the oven to 400 degrees. Place 12 cupcake liners on a baking sheet and set aside until ready to use.

2 In a small mixing bowl, combine all ingredients except the potatoes. Mix well and transfer to a large zip-close plastic bag. Add potatoes, seal shut, and shake to cover potato skins with herb oil.

3 Place each coated potato inside a cupcake liner. Discard any remaining oil. Bake for 30–45 minutes or until fork tender.

4 Remove potatoes from oven, let cool for 10 minutes, and cut potatoes in half. Add toppings of choice and serve warm or at room temperature.

These are incredibly tasty, but the odds of successfully navigating an asteroid field are still woefully against you.

PLUTONIAN PIZZAS

1 Using the recipe for Breadstick Blasters, add a small amount of blue paste food coloring to the water. Mix well and proceed with recipe directions.

2 Preheat the oven to 375 degrees. Line a cookie sheet with parchment paper and set aside until ready to use.

3 Divide the dough into 6 balls and flatten into circles with your hands. Place on the prepared sheet pan. Spread each dough circle with 1/2 teaspoon pesto and top with mozzarella cheese slices.

4 Bake for 10–15 minutes or until the cheese is melted and the crust is very lightly browned.

INGREDIENTS

1 recipe Breadstick Blasters Dough (page 15)

Blue paste food coloring

Purchased pesto

6 Mozzarella cheese slices

MAKES 6 6-INCH PIZZAS

Raffaele Esposito created the first pizza in Italy, Earth, in 1889. Since then, it has become an intergalactic favorite, with 50,000 new franchises opening galaxy-wide every month. Plutonians from Pluto have since disputed Esposito's claim, and the matter is being settled in superior court. If you ever have lunch with a Plutonian, it's best to just order the calzone.

WORMHOLE ROLL-UPS

INGREDIENTS

4 cups fresh spinach

1/4 cup water or low-sodium vegetable broth

1 (15-ounce) can cannellini beans

2 tablespoons lemon juice (from about 1 lemon)

1/4 cup tahini

1 clove garlic

1/8 teaspoon fine sea salt

4 whole grain tortillas

1 avocado, thinly sliced

1/2 cucumber, peeled and very thinly sliced

1 small red bell pepper, very thinly sliced

MAKES 16
ROLL-UPS

1 Place spinach, water or broth, beans, lemon juice, tahini, garlic, and salt in a food processor and pulse until smooth to make hummus.

2 Spread about 2 tablespoons hummus on 1 tortilla, leaving about an inch from the edge uncovered. Arrange 1/4 each of sliced avocado, sliced cucumber, and sliced bell pepper on top of hummus, and tightly roll up tortilla.

3 Repeat with the remaining tortillas, hummus, avocado, cucumber, and bell pepper. Carefully cut each wrapped tortilla into four pinwheels.

> Wormholes have a habit of showing up at the most inconvenient times. Like in the middle of a galactic battle. Or your afternoon tea.
>
> It's hard to say which is worse.

RAVIOLI

1 Follow manufacturer's directions for cooking the ravioli; drain the ravioli and place it on a plate.

2 Drizzle the ravioli with Mars Marinara Sauce and garnish with grated cheese, if desired.

MARS MARINARA SAUCE

1 Heat olive oil in a medium saucepan over medium heat. Add garlic and cook, stirring often, until it begins to lightly brown, roughly 1–2 minutes.

2 Lower heat and add tomato puree. Stir in maple syrup, and season with sea salt and pepper to taste.

3 Bring to a boil, reduce heat, and simmer gently until the mixture has slightly thickened, roughly 10–15 minutes.

Sauce may be refrigerated for up to 1 week or frozen for up to 3 months prior to use.

> The first red alert system was developed by the commander of the *Carmellion* battlecruiser, whose crew was, unfortunately, completely color blind.

INGREDIENTS

RAVIOLI

1 (12-ounce) package ravioli*

Mars Marinara Sauce

1/4 cup grated parmesan or mozzarella cheese (optional)

MAKES 4 SERVINGS

SAUCE

1/4 cup olive oil

2 garlic cloves, chopped

1 (28-ounce) can pureed tomatoes

1/4 teaspoon maple syrup

Sea salt and pepper

MAKES ROUGHLY 4 CUPS

*We used 100 percent Natural Jolie Rav
Visit www.nyravioli.com/jolie.htm

BURRITO BOWL BOOSTERS

INGREDIENTS

3 cups brown rice, cooked

1 lime, juiced

1 tablespoon olive oil

1/3 cup fresh cilantro, chopped

Corn chips for base of bowl (optional)

1 (15-ounce) can black beans, drained and rinsed

2 cups shredded chicken (2 medium chicken breasts)

2 avocados, lightly mashed with a little salt and pepper

3/4 cup salsa

1/2 cup plain Greek yogurt

Fresh corn, chopped tomatoes, cheddar cheese (optional)

MAKES 6 BURRITO BOWLS

1 Place rice in a large bowl. Add lime juice, olive oil, and fresh cilantro. Toss to blend.

2 Place corn chips, if desired, in the bottom of 6 shallow bowls.

3 Divide the rice between the bowls and top with black beans.

4 Add shredded chicken and a layer of mashed avocado.

5 Top with salsa and Greek yogurt. Finish with additional toppings of your choice.

Nothing prepares you for defending your galaxy against an invasion of mutant aliens like the good old burrito bowl. But please, let your food settle at least 15 minutes before saving the world. Doctor's orders.

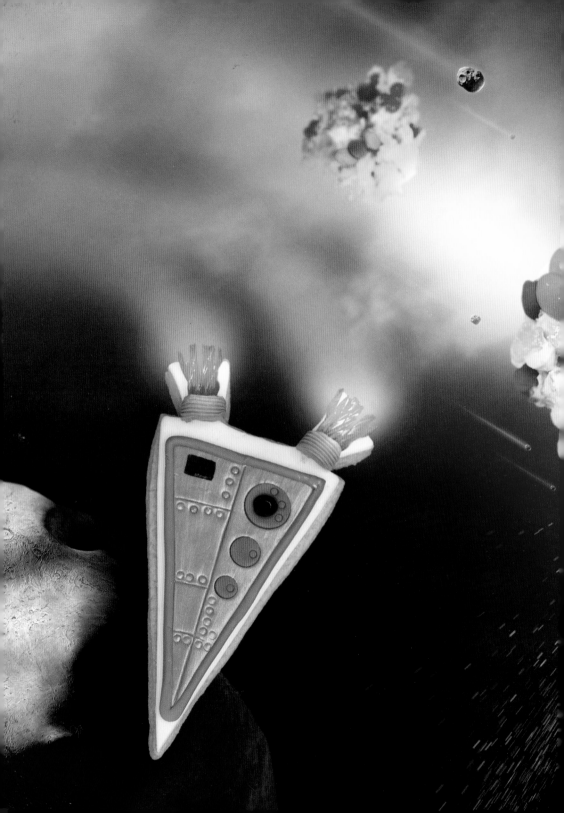

SECTOR 3

SWEETS
& TREATS

ORBITAL ICING

1 Place the butter in a large mixing bowl. Add 6 cups of powdered sugar and all of the milk. Beat for 3–5 minutes. Continue adding powdered sugar in increments of 2 cups at a time, beating well after each addition. You may not need all the powdered sugar.

2 Add the vanilla and mix well.

3 Using an electric mixer on medium speed, beat the frosting until it is smooth and creamy. Add your favorite color of food coloring and mix until well combined.

CAKE

1 Preheat oven to 350 degrees. Generously spray 2 sphere cake pans with cooking oil. You may also bake a sphere cake in 2 heavy-gauge stainless steel mixing bowls. Nest the cake pans or bowls inside 2 regular round cake pans to ensure they sit level throughout the baking process.

2 Set aside until ready to use.

SPACE HERO HELPFUL HINT:
We used Fat Daddio's 8x4-inch sphere cake pan. Visit
http://amzn.com/B001VEI0AQ

INGREDIENTS

_____

ORBITAL ICING

2 cups (4 sticks) unsalted butter, softened

2 pounds powdered sugar

4–6 tablespoons whole milk

1 tablespoon vanilla extract

Food coloring, any color

CAKE

4 boxes vanilla or white cake mixes

Eggs, as many as the 4 cake mixes require

Food colorings: yellow, turquoise, electric green, orange, and purple

Astronautic Icing

Fondants, assorted colors

Edible glitter or luster dust

SERVES 12–15

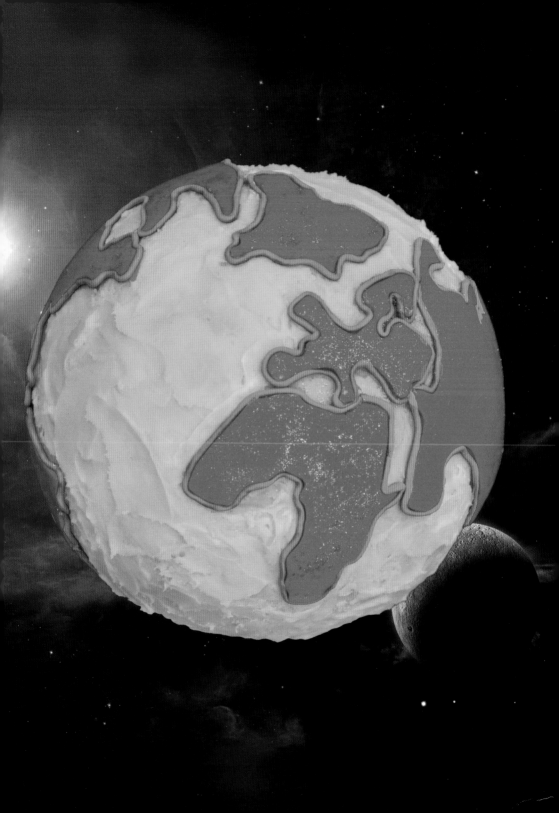

3 Make 2 cake mixes at a time, following the manufacturer's directions. Divide the combined batter from the first two boxes evenly between 5 bowls and add different colors of food coloring to each one, mixing well to combine. Fill one sphere with batter colors, slowly pouring one on top of the other until all 5 colors are used.

4 Make a second batch of batter, repeat the procedure, and fill the second sphere.

5 Place the cake pans in the oven and bake for 35–45 minutes or until light golden brown and a toothpick inserted into the center comes out clean.

6 Remove cakes from the oven and place the pans on a wire rack to cool for 1 hour (or until pan is cool to the touch) before unmolding.

CAKE CONSTRUCTION

1 Remove the cakes from their pans. Frost the flat side of each cake and then fit the flat sides together. Smooth over the seam with more frosting. Place the completed sphere in the refrigerator for 30 minutes to allow the frosting to harden.

2 Remove from the refrigerator. Use a knife to take a thin slice off the bottom of the sphere to allow it to sit on a flat surface. Frost the full exterior of the sphere. Place in refrigerator again to chill while cutting out fondant continents.

3 Roll out fondants and cut them into continent shapes. Embellish with glitter dust or luster dust.

SPACE HERO HELPFUL HINT:
We used *Feed the World Cookie Cutters* found on Amazon.com for the continent cut-outs. Visit http://amzn.com/B00863CHEO

4 Remove the cake from the refrigerator and apply the fondants.

Store uncovered for up to one day.

1. Preheat the oven to 325 degrees. Line a cupcake pan with liners and set aside until ready to use.

2. Add all the dry ingredients to a large mixing bowl and mix together thoroughly with a whisk.

3. Add the wet ingredients to the bowl and beat with an electric mixer on low. Then increase the speed and mix on high for 2 more minutes.

4. Fill cupcake liners 2/3 full and bake for 15–20 minutes.

5. Remove from the oven and cool in pans for 5 minutes before removing and completely cooling on a wire rack. Then frost the cupcakes and decorate them with chocolate rock candies.

SPACE HERO HELPFUL HINT:
We used Kimmie Candy Company's Chocolate Rocks Candy Nuggets. Visit http://amzn.com/B0084Y9CLC

> Moon rocks are difficult to distinguish from moon zocks, which are similar in size but have eyes, mouths, and a voracious appetite for humans. We recommend staying away from both.

INGREDIENTS

1 box cake mix, any flavor

1 cup all-purpose flour

1 cup granulated sugar

1 cup water

3 eggs, room temperature

1 cup sour cream

2 teaspoons pure vanilla extract

1 recipe Orbital Icing (page 32)

Chocolate rock candies

MAKES 24
CUPCAKES

SMUGGLERS' CUPCAKES

INGREDIENTS

1 box chocolate cake mix

1 cup buttermilk, in place of water called for on the box

4 eggs, in place of the number called for on the box

Vegetable oil, same as the amount on the box

2–3 cups M&Ms®

1 recipe Orbital Icing (page 32)

Fondant and pearl luster dust

MAKES 24 CUPCAKES

1 Preheat the oven to 350 degrees. Line a muffin pan with paper liners. Set aside until ready to use.

2 Follow the cake mix directions, using 1 cup buttermilk instead of water and using 4 eggs. Combine all the ingredients in a large bowl.

3 Beat with an electric mixer until moistened, about 30 seconds. Increase the speed to high and beat until thick, about 2 minutes.

4 Fill paper liners 2/3 full and bake 15–20 minutes.

5 Remove the cupcakes from the oven and allow them to cool completely.

6 Gently core out a small hole from each cupcake with a paring knife or apple corer. Fill each hole with M&Ms®.

7 Using a piping bag fitted with a large star tip, frost each cupcake (this will easily cover and hide the little secret hole).

8 Cut out fondant stars with a small cookie cutter and apply pearl luster dust with a small clean paintbrush. Top each cupcake with a star.

> Smugglers are fast, elusive, and have more pockets than a Zabinthian kangaroo. They also have an obsession with cupcakes, so inspect those first.

INTERSTELLAR SPACE FIGHTER COOKIES

COOKIES

1 Preheat the oven to 375 degrees. Line 2 baking sheets with parchment paper. Set aside until ready to use.

2 Cream the butter in a large mixing bowl with an electric mixer. Slowly add sugar, beating until light and fluffy. Add the egg and vanilla, mixing well.

3 Combine flour, baking soda, and salt in a separate bowl. Add to the creamed mixture, blending well. The dough will be very stiff.

4 Cut the dough with a rocket cookie cutter. Insert a candy stick or Popsicle® stick into each cut-out, if desired.

5 Place the cookies on the prepared backing sheet and bake for 10 minutes or until lightly browned.

6 Remove the cookies from the oven and all them to cool on the baking sheet for 5 minutes before transferring them to a wire rack to cool completely. Then frost and decorate the cookies.

DECORATING

1 Cut base fondant color using the same rocket cookie cutter that was used to shape the sugar cookies. Using a tiny bit of icing, adhere each cut-out to the cookies.

INGREDIENTS

SUGAR COOKIES

1/2 cup (1 stick) butter, softened

3/4 cup sugar

1 egg

1 teaspoon vanilla

2 cups flour

1/2 teaspoon baking soda

1/4 teaspoon salt

12 candy or Popsicle® sticks

COOKIE DECORATING

Fondants, assorted colors

Orbital Icing (page 32) or 1 can prepared vanilla icing

Twizzlers®

Luster dust

MAKES A DOZEN 3-INCH COOKIES

2 In a contrasting color of fondant, outline a triangle 1/4 inch inside the edge of the fondant cutout.

3 Using luster dust and a small paintbrush, color the inside of the fondant outline.

4 Use a small wooden skewer to press lines and adornments onto the fondant. Use the end of a straw to form small circles for portholes.

5 Using another fondant color, form three small circles of varying sizes and place on rocket with a bit of icing.

6 For the burning engines, form two small amounts of fondant into 1/2-inch pieces. Draw a few lines onto each piece with a wooden skewer and adhere the pieces to the cookie with a bit of icing.

7 Cut Twizzlers® into 1-inch lengths and adhere underneath each of the cookie "engines" with a little icing.

History's largest space battle was the invasion of Laforte in 3468 AD. There were too many ships to maneuver properly, however, so everyone gave up and had history's largest picnic instead.

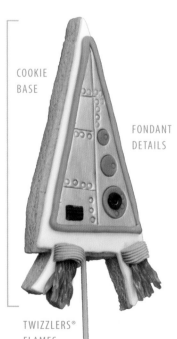

COOKIE BASE

FONDANT DETAILS

TWIZZLERS® FLAMES

RINGS OF SATURN DONUT POPS

INGREDIENTS

1 teaspoon apple cider vinegar or white vinegar

2/3 cup milk of choice

1 teaspoon pure vanilla extract

2 1/2 tablespoons vegetable or melted coconut oil

1 cup all-purpose flour

1 1/2 teaspoons baking powder

1/2 cup sugar

1/4 teaspoon salt

1 pound white vanilla candy coating

Powdered or oil-based food coloring*

20 cake pop sticks

Fondants, assorted colors

Egg carton

MAKES 18-20 DONUT POPS

* Water-based liquid or paste food coloring will seize the candy coating and ruin the texture.

SPACE HERO HELPFUL HINT:
If you don't have time to make donut holes, you can purchase cake donut holes.

1 Preheat the oven to 350 degrees, and lightly spray a donut hole pan with cooking spray. Set aside until ready to use.

2 In a small bowl, whisk together the vinegar, milk, vanilla, and oil. In a large bowl whisk together the flour, baking powder, sugar, and salt.

3 Pour the wet ingredients into the dry ingredients and stir until just evenly mixed. Divide the batter evenly between the cavities in the donut hole pan.

SPACE HERO HELPFUL HINT:
We used the Wilton Donut Hole Cake Pan.
Visit http://amzn.com/B00C9MRQF4

4 Bake 7–8 minutes. Remove from oven and cool completely before removing from pan.

5 While the donut holes are cooling, turn the empty egg carton upside down and use a cake pop stick to poke a hole into each cup. Set aside until ready to use. This will serve as a drying stand later on.

6 Melt the candy coating according to the package directions. Divide the melted coating evenly between two bowls and add food coloring of choice to each of the bowls, mixing well to blend. It's best to have two contrasting colors.

43

7 In a third bowl, pour half of the first color and half of the second color. Stir the two colors just slightly to created a swirled, marbled pattern. Be careful not to over stir.

8 To secure the donut holes to the cake pop sticks, dip one end of each stick into the candy coating and insert the dipped end into a donut hole. Once the stick and donut hole are connected, place each pop on a foil-covered cookie sheet and allow to dry for 5–10 minutes.

9 Once the donut pops are dry, dip each pop into the swirled candy coating. Tap the stick gently on the side of the bowl to remove any extra coating from the pop. Stand each cake pop stick in one of the holes in the egg carton and allow to dry completely.

10 When you run out of the marbled mixture, repeat step 7 with the remaining candy coating to make another batch.

11 Create "Saturn Rings" by mixing together 3 colors of fondant to create a swirl effect. Flatten the fondant with a rolling pin and cut out rings to fit each pop.

12 Allow the fondant rings to air dry 15–20 minutes before placing on coated pops.

Store in the refrigerator and serve within 24 hours.

Saturn's rings puzzled astronomers for centuries until closer inspection revealed that they were just the practice facility of the Titan track and field team. Titans have dominated the 1,000,000 km sprint for the past 40 years.

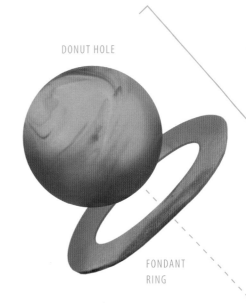

DONUT HOLE

FONDANT RING

COMET CRUNCH POPCORN BALLS

1. Cover a baking sheet with parchment paper. Set aside until ready to use.

2. Place popped corn in a large bowl. Set aside until ready to assemble.

3. Melt the butter and marshmallows in a large pot over medium heat, stirring constantly, until marshmallows are melted and mixture is smooth.

4. Remove the mixture from heat and add vanilla and food coloring, stirring well to mix in food coloring.

5. Pour the mixture on top of the popcorn and toss with a wooden spoon until marshmallow mixture is evenly distributed. Pour sprinkles liberally over popcorn and stir once more.

6. Spray your hands with non-stick spray and grab a large handful of popcorn mixture. Roll the mixture gently into a ball about 2–3 inches thick. Continue making balls until all the popcorn is used.

7. To decorate the popcorn balls, roll them in sprinkles or candy decorations.

8. To add marshmallow decorations, melt 1 square (about 1 ounce) of candy coating in the microwave according to package directions. Dip one end of each mini marshmallow into melted coating and dip into colored sugar or sprinkles. Use a dab of candy coating to adhere the marshmallows to the popcorn balls.

INGREDIENTS

2 cups popped popcorn

1/4 cup salted butter

1 10-ounce bag marshmallows

1 teaspoon vanilla

Food coloring

Sprinkles, colored sugars, mini marshmallows, and candy decorations (sprinkles, M&Ms®, etc.)

White (vanilla) candy coating

MAKES A DOZEN 2-INCH POPCORN BALLS

SECTOR 4

DRINKS

1. In a large container, combine blue sports drink with 1/4 teaspoon of edible glitter. Stir to combine.

2. Cut strawberries into chunks and apples into stars.

3. Garnish with strawberries and star-shaped apple slices.

INGREDIENTS

1 (32-ounce) bottle blue sports drink, chilled

1/4 teaspoon edible glitter

Strawberries and apples, for garnish

MAKES 12
SERVINGS

LASER BEAM LEMONADE

INGREDIENTS

---

2 cups sugar

2 cups water

1 gallon cold water

2 cups fresh lemon juice

MAKES 12
SERVINGS

1 Combine sugar and water in a medium saucepan. Bring to a boil over low heat. Stir until the sugar dissolves and then remove the mixture from heat. Set aside to cool.

2 To serve, add a gallon of cold water and lemon juice to a large glass container. Add the simple syrup and stir well. Serve ice-cold with colorful straws.

SPACE HERO HELPFUL HINT:
Simple syrup may be made several days ahead and chilled in the refrigerator for up to one week.

When combined and amplified, turbolasers have enough power to destroy entire suns and planets. They can also make a perfectly roasted hot dog—crispy on the outside, warm the whole way through. Mmmm.

1 Combine juice and sparkling water in a large container and serve in a smaller serving bowl.

2 For dry ice presentation, place the serving bowl (with the punch inside) in a larger bowl. Fill the space between the bowls with chunks of dry ice. Keep this out of reach of little hands; the dry ice will burn skin quickly.

1 (46-ounce) bottle grape juice, chilled

1 (1-liter) bottle sparkling water, chilled

Dry ice (optional)

MAKES 12 SERVINGS

When dealing with space pirates, remember their three biggest weaknesses: pirate punch, nonsensical monologues, and all-you-can-eat Tresperian buffets (the bread pudding is to die for).

APOLLO'S APPLE JUICE

INGREDIENTS

6 cups apple juice or apple cider, chilled

2 cups orange juice or orange juice blend such as mango/orange, chilled

2 cups 100 percent lemonade (or Laser Beam Lemonade, page 53), chilled

Orange slices, for garnish

MAKES 12 SERVINGS

1 Combine all ingredients in a large serving container.

2 Serve and garnish with orange slices.

Apollo is the name of a Greek god, a series of lunar missions, and the best juice bar in the Gamma sector. Just don't order the Sonorian Smoothie . . . you've been warned.

SPACE CADET QUENCHER

1 Combine ingredients in a large serving container.

2 Garnish with kiwi slices.

INGREDIENTS

1 (59-ounce) bottle 100 percent limeade (or Laser Beam Lemonade; substitute lime juice for lemon juice), chilled

1 (32-ounce) bottle bright green sports drink, chilled

Kiwi slices, for garnish

MAKES 12 SERVINGS

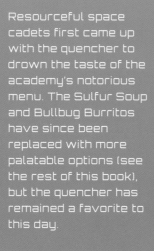

Resourceful space cadets first came up with the quencher to drown the taste of the academy's notorious menu. The Sulfur Soup and Bullbug Burritos have since been replaced with more palatable options (see the rest of this book), but the quencher has remained a favorite to this day.

WARP CORE COOLER

INGREDIENTS

1 (64-ounce) bottle 100 percent cherry pomegranate juice (or your favorite cherry juice blend), chilled

Fresh strawberries, sliced

Whipped cream, for garnish

Silver edible glitter, for garnish

MAKES 12 SERVINGS

1 Combine the chilled juice and fresh strawberry slices in a large serving container.

2 Serve each drink with a dollop of whipped cream and a sprinkling of silver glitter.

SPACE HERO HELPFUL HINT:
We used CK Products edible Silver Glitter Dust to garnish our drink. Find it at Michael's or at http://amzn.com/B00CRJ68GM

> Warp drives can be powered by several different materials, including plasma, antimatter, and, curiously enough, fermented orange juice.

SECTOR 5

CRAFTS

SPACE SLUG SLIME

1. Combine the glue, 1 cup of warm water, and food coloring in a bowl and mix well.

2. In another bowl, combine 1/2 cup of warm water with the borax. Mix well.

3. Pour the borax mixture into the glue mixture and stir with a spoon until it creates a slime.

Store in a covered container for up to 2 weeks.

SPACE HERO HELPFUL HINT:
For the success of the recipe, the glue must be the Elmer's brand; no substitutes. Also, borax can be found in any major grocery store in the laundry detergent section.

INGREDIENTS

1 cup Elmer's Glue

1 cup warm water

Paste food coloring, any color

1/2 cup warm water

1 teaspoon borax

MAKES ONE 6-8-INCH "GLOB"

Space slugs are odorous, destructive, quick to anger, and larger than a Talorian skybus.

We recommend crossing to the other side of the street.

ANTIGRAVITY CHALK

INGREDIENTS

Tempera paint, any color

1 cup water

1 1/2 cups Plaster of Paris

Mixing spoon

Assorted silicone molds, any shape

MAKES 4-5 PIECES
OF CHALK

1 In a plastic container, mix 2–4 tablespoons (depending on color desired) of paint into the water.

2 Continue mixing while slowly adding the Plaster of Paris to the water until completely combined. The mixture should be about the texture of frosting.

3 Fill molds with the mixture. Tap the molds lightly to release air bubbles.

4 Allow the plaster to set for about 1 hour before removing the chalk pieces from the molds. (Check for hardness by gently squeezing each mold.)

5 Place the individual chalk pieces on a rack and allow them to dry for 24 hours before using them.

SPACE HERO HELPFUL HINT:
Plaster of Paris can be found in most arts and craft stores.

1. In a small bowl, add 1/8 teaspoon black paste food coloring to the water and mix well. Add the oil and set aside until ready to use.

2. Pour the dry ingredients into a saucepan and whisk to combine. Gradually add the water mixture and stir to combine with a wooden spoon.

3. Cook over medium heat, stirring, until a dough ball forms. Remove from heat.

4. Turn out dough onto a clean work surface, sprinkle with glitter, sequins, or stars, and knead until glitter is incorporated.

Cool and store in an airtight container for up to one month.

INGREDIENTS

Black paste food coloring

1 cup water

2 tablespoons vegetable oil

1 1/2 cups all-purpose flour

1/2 cup salt

2 tablespoons cream of tartar

2–3 tablespoons silver, purple, and blue glitter

Sequins or small stars

MAKES ONE 6-8-INCH "GLOB"

For convenience, meteorites are usually grouped into 6 classes:

1—Dwarf
2—Small
3—Medium
4—Large
5—What the . . .
6—TURN THIS SHIP AROUND!

CARBONITE CRAYONS

INGREDIENTS

Crayons, assorted colors, broken into small pieces (a great way to use old crayons)

Assorted silicone molds

4-5 CRAYONS MAKE ONE 2-INCH MOLD

1 Preheat the oven to 175 degrees.

2 Fill molds to the top with broken crayons. Place molds on a baking sheet and bake just until the wax has melted (about 15–20 minutes, depending on the size of the molds).

3 Remove from the oven and cool completely, about 30 minutes, before removing from molds.

SPACE HERO HELPFUL HINT:
We used glitter and metallic Crayola Crayons to make our crayons out of this world!

Anything made from carbonite keeps good indefinitely, but it has an uncanny habit of attracting bounty hunters of the worst repute. Use with caution.

GAMMA RAY GLOW JARS

1 Paint small dots all over the inside of each jar with the paint. Allow to the painted jars to dry without lids for 15 minutes.

2 Squirt a small amount of paint into the bottom of each jar, secure lids, and turn jars upside down to create a swirl effect with the paint. Turn right-side up again and remove lids to allow paint to dry completely for another 30 minutes.

3 Place directly under a lamp or near a light bulb for at least 30 minutes (ask a grown-up to assist).

4 Secure lids, turn off the lights, and let it glow!

5 Sealed jars may be recharged and used for up to one year.

SPACE HERO HELPFUL HINT:
We used glass mason jars, but we do not recommend using glass if children will be decorating them as a craft. For a great selection of plastic jars, we love the Sugar Diva: bit.ly/1BZDTZK

Glow jars are wonderfully useful when you find yourself in a tight spot—like the stomach of a space slug. (You really should have followed our advice on page 64.)

INGREDIENTS

12 (12-ounce) plastic jars with lids

Glow-in-the-dark paint

Small paint brush

DECORATES A DOZEN 12-OUNCE JARS

SUPERNOVA SOAPS

INGREDIENTS

1 pound clear glycerin melt

Liquid soaps, three different colors

Silicone mold (round ice cube mold, chocolate or soap mold, etc.)

MAKES 15–18 BARS OF SOAP

1 Heat the glycerin over low heat in a saucepan or in a microwave safe dish according to package directions.

2 Remove from heat and squirt a few drops of each of the three liquid soaps separately into each mold.

3 Using a small spouted measuring cup or pitcher, pour glycerin into each mold. Wipe off any glycerin from the outside of the mold before cooling.

4 Place molds in the refrigerator to chill for at least 1 hour. Remove from the refrigerator and unmold.

SPACE HERO HELPFUL HINT: Some holes in the molds may be too small for pouring in the glycerin. Simply cut a slightly larger hole with scissors to allow easier flow of glycerin. Round ice cube molds are very popular. Check out this resource for a great selection: amzn.to/1EXhhet.

Over the course of your space hero career, you will be ingested by aliens, trapped in trash compactors, and covered in every variety of primordial glop, gook, and gunk known to man.

Soap is not optional.

1   In a large mixing bowl, combine flour and tempera paint powder.

2   Mix with a whisk to combine and add baby oil. Mix together with a wooden spoon and use your hands, too!

3   The texture should feel crumbly but moldable when squeezed. Add a little more flour if the mixture feels too damp. Or add a teaspoon (or more) of baby oil if it does not hold together well.

4   Store in an airtight container for up to 2 weeks.

INGREDIENTS

9 cups all-purpose flour

2 tablespoons powdered tempera paint

1 1/4 cup baby oil

MAKES ABOUT 10 CUPS

Moon sand can't protect you from lasers, solar blasts, or self-inflicted wounds. But if you're sick of solitaire, it does wonders for interplanetary flights.

CONVERSIONS

VOLUME MEASUREMENTS

U.S.	METRIC
1 teaspoon	5 ml
1 tablespoon	15 ml
1/4 cup	60 ml
1/3 cup	75 ml
1/2 cup	125 ml
2/3 cup	150 ml
3/4 cup	175 ml
1 cup	250 ml

WEIGHT MEASUREMENTS

U.S.	METRIC
1/2 ounce	15 g
1 ounce	30 g
3 ounces	90g
4 ounces	115 g
8 ounces	225 g
12 ounces	350 g
1 pound	450 g
2 1/4 pounds	1 kg

TEMPERATURE CONVERSION

FAHRENHEIT	CELSIUS
250	120
300	150
325	160
350	180
375	190
400	200
425	220
450	230

MEET BARBARA

Barbara Beery, the bestselling author of *The Pink Princess Cookbook*, has been a spokesperson for such national companies as Sun-Maid Raisin, Uncle Ben's, Borden's, Kellogg's Rice Krispies, and Step 2. Barbara has been a contributing writer to *FamilyFun*, the country's leading family magazine. She has appeared twice on the *Today Show* and CBN with Pat Robertson. Beery's business has been featured in the *New York Times* and *Entrepreneur* magazine, as well as dozens of other local and national publications. She has worked closely with Get Moving, Cookies for Kids Cancer, Rachael Ray's Yum-o! Organization, and No Kids Hungry.

Barbara is the author of 12 books, having sold more than 500,000 copies. She resides in Austin, Texas.

ABOUT FOODIE KIDS

Foodie Kids is the largest and most unique kids culinary center in the country. It includes a cooking school, retail store, and The Makery®, a drop-in make-your-own snack counter.

The center started as a series of cooking classes in Barbara's home kitchen twenty-five years ago. Through the years, the small cooking school grew into an operation that was no longer manageable to operate from her home. With years of hard work, the small cottage business turned into a retail culinary destination for kids and families to celebrate birthdays, take cooking classes, host field trips, and enjoy summer cooking camps.

For more information, visit www.foodie-kids.com.

ABOUT FAMILIUS

Welcome to a place where mothers are celebrated, not compared. Where heart is at the center of our families, and family at the center of our homes. Where boo-boos are still kissed, cake beaters are still licked, and mistakes are still okay. Welcome to a place where books—and family—are beautiful. Familius: a book publisher dedicated to helping families be happy.

VISIT OUR WEBSITE: WWW.FAMILIUS.COM

Our website is a different kind of place. Get inspired, read articles, discover books, watch videos, connect with our family experts, download books and apps and audiobooks, and along the way, discover how values and happy family life go together.

JOIN OUR FAMILY

There are lots of ways to connect with us! Subscribe to our newsletters at www.familius.com to receive uplifting daily inspiration, essays from our Pater Familius, a free ebook every month, and the first word on special discounts and Familius news.

GET BULK DISCOUNTS

If you feel a few friends and family might benefit from what you've read, let us know and we'll be happy to provide you with quantity discounts. Simply email us at specialorders@familius.com.

Website: www.familius.com
Facebook: www.facebook.com/paterfamilius
Twitter: @familiustalk, @paterfamilius1
Pinterest: www.pinterest.com/familius

FAMILIUS

DEC 2016